Dreams Within Dreams

RED EGG

Jean Bonnin

Jean Bonnin

Jean Bonnin was born in Lavaur, in the Tarn in France. He is a novelist, poet, artist, and musician who now lives in South West Wales.

Dreams Within Dreams
An Original Publication of Red Egg
Publishing
An imprint of Red Egg International
First published in the UK by Red Egg
Publishing
in 2018
www.redeggpublishing.com

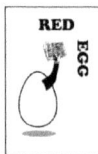

Cover design: Red Egg Publishing

*British Library Cataloguing-in-Publication
Data*

A catalogue record for this book is available upon request from the British Library

ISBN: 978-1-9998215-1-7

Contents

Time's Last Cigarette

Time took its cigarette
And stubbed it out on the palm of our
hands
Stardust souvenirs written on blue
paper
For unknown moments and
unforeseen adventures

In a parallel universe I am writing
something else
As low lighting beckons the night in
And we travel to Turkey and back
again
As we travel to Berlin and then back
again

Turn around turn around and turn
around again
So I can consider you as flick-book
pinhole moments

Moments caught on celluloid for
crystal dances
As chandeliers writhe like Japanese
symbols playing underwater

Down to earth, you're so down to
earth
And I'm down on you
We're like holograms encased in
concrete
We shall sing as we used to do
And recall that parachutes are not
required
For jumping into puddles

In the distance the woman in loosely
spun cotton
Cries to the realisation that she is
suddenly aware
Aware of love and death, alcohol and
angels
And aware... aware that I've put her in
this poem

Shattered Waves

The crescent moon shattered waves
Shine behind her smile
As she rushes to the backdoor
Of her own private hell

In a thousand forgotten moments
Are a thousand discarded hopes
As the stinging-lipped streets
Seep from her strawberry lips

Lamp-lit broken bus-stop
And a ketchup-stained carton
Boarded up buildings
In the piss-stained streets

Her past she cannot escape from
As she walks towards the tree
And the future is always tomorrow
Unless you die today

Car screech and the pavements bleed
On the rain-bleached streets

The death of a loved one
In the autumn sun

The Seahorses of Time

With my lighted cigarette
I can see the moon

With my turned up collar
I won't fall in line

As we shall loose our memories
On the seashores of time

Floating Bird

Joy is a three-letter word
Suck it up
Like a floating bird
Soft-wing in duvet flight
On feathers of breeze
So soothing
Wrap-around vortex
Personality codex
Light foot shuffle shoe
And the eased calm of a gentle sea
Floating down to the ground
On wafts
Wafts and wafers
Thin as pancakes
Sucking-up
Sucked-up
Splendid moments
Loved-up
Like a matryoshka doll
Wrapped in a blini blanket
On a honey-river of snowflakes

Lascaux

It is too wide
Too large
The expanse of time
And the calm breathing of the
Universe
Like hibernating giants gently snoring
The past away

Colours and drawing too exquisite to
comprehend
From before everything began
From before the rising of the first sun
almost
This is how it feels
In the presence of such perfection
For it is perfect
Perfect in its un-knowability
Perfect in its creation and its
imagination

Galloping across the walls to reach our
eyes
To be perceived by our foreign gaze
To fashion questions into our mouths
As we throw sand into the eyes of the
disbelievers

Here is proof
If proof were needed
That art and time
Like memories
Are carved from the same rock

Pulse

Weepfulness
And craziness
Of doubtful haze
Coming from the moon
Pulsating
Down
Its disturbance

As the
Gentle
Breeze
Of infinity
Caresses
Through
My hair

Surrealist Love Song

Lucifer, Blackbird, Dodo, Moo
The chiselled sunrise for me and you
Lucifer, Blackbird, Dodo, Moo
I can't read the signals of what to do

Flattering car-crash, partridge fuss
The answer's in the question,
beansprout, bust
Flattering car-crash, ball-bearing fuss
And there's silence all around us

I wrote a surrealist love song for thee
Clatter, bang, wallop, sandwich full of
Brie
I wrote a surrealist poem for you
Skip over fences in an elephant's shoe

Tu est le pain dans ma soupe
Le vent dans mon prout
La mèche dans ma bougie
Et le sourire sur ma souris

T'es l'aile d'un l'oiseau
La gorge d'un crapaud
Les œufs dans mon omelette
T'es le 'corn' á mon 'pop'

Monkey, minkey, cloudburst, whoosh
Lazy stream, staring at the sky
Cloud formations, lobster, fish
Sunlight ripples as afternoon sighs

Le monde est bleu comme une orange
Brille de longs éclairs
J'embrassé l'aube d'été
Car Les rêves sont la littérature du
sommeil

Sit upon my magic falafel
Pita bread – when all's done and said
Sit upon my magic falafel baby
Chilli sauce – but of course

Will you share a glass of beer – my
dear
With a bear and a deer – my dear

Let's make love on a giant telephone –
my dear
Cos I wrote a surrealist song for you
my dear

Sipping From Rivers

Curry houses and the Underground
And a loaf of Polish bread
For a picnic by the river
In the shadow of the Globe and Tate
Modern
Sitting with my lover eating
Sandwiches in the sun

And I don't feel afraid
'Cos I can see the sky from where I am
As the night turns on the lights
And the sun bends down to sip the
river

Divinely Imperfect

Strangle me in your effervescent glow
Love of chaos
And jumble dance light swirls
Your spirit
Moulded from distant light
Shoots past my skylight
On its journey to the moon

Silver webs on rain-glistened morning
Vibrating in the gentle breeze
Like prisms of pyramids
Shattering light into its component
parts
So I have become a child
Held tight in the presence of magic

Electricity comes from other planets
Your power is unknown to you
Breathing sparks into the flames
Sunlight in the shadows
And paintings onto the walls of caves

You are the immortality of tribal
chants

Divinely imperfect
Beautifully ambiguous
A creature of legend and myth

Esmeralda
(a.k.a.)

She plunged callously
Her decaying talons
Into his concentration camp ribcage
Pulling out life itself
To devour it
In the most detached and
choreographed of feeding frenzies

Throwing the universe up in the air
Strapping destruction to her body
And exploding art and love
Into smithereens
As the black sun that became her halo
Glowered its deformed light
Over the scene

And so she ate on...
And then when her
Catatonia had

Screamed its ugliness
Over those once
Pristine
Starfish sands
She neatly aligned
The debris
Into lines and columns
Chiselling away
An unfathomable
Orderliness
Out of destruction

And then she swallowed triumphantly
And left

I Remember

I remember Mr Benn
I remember building a den
I remember bonfire night
And I remember Mr Wilson's pipe

I remember the Blue Peter appeal
I remember the teatime meal
I remember the four minute warning
And I remember Tis Was in the
morning

The days when terrorists were noble
When we supported freedom fighters
across the world
When we were fighting for coal not
dole
And when Socialism seemed an
achievable goal
The S.L.A. seemed one solution

The Poll Tax riots and destroying
Thatcher's revolution
We were waiting for a brighter
tomorrow
And thought that things could never
get worse than they were then

I remember the Clash at number 1
I remember the hot summer sun
I remember hating the Queen
And, I remember hating Queen

I remember Spike Milligan's Q
I remember 3 million having nothing
to do
I remember Greenham Common
And how the Belgrano will never be
forgotten

I remember watching final score
I remember the wolf at the door
I remember The Tube and George
Best

And I remember The Old Grey Whistle
Test

It was the days when terrorists were
noble
When we supported freedom fighters
across the world
When we were fighting for coal not
dole
And when Anarchism seemed an
achievable goal
Communal living seemed one solution
The Poll Tax riots and destroying
Thatcher's revolution
We were waiting for a brighter
tomorrow
And things can never get worse than
they are NOW

Cruiser

The cars on the road
Are like aliens in stockings
Monosodium glutamate
Like chicken stock
Gridlock
Pickpock padlock
New York New York
Buy some new stock
For a brighter future
A whiter cruiser
A life switch
With bright teeth
Spinning on a sixpence
To find tuppence
Where tone reflects your home
And the car's in your slot
On a pain and glass plot
As we throttle the bugler
On a sunblast morning
In a row
All little ducks in a row

Where difference
Is the individuality
Of sameness

André Breton

Life, time
Bohemian

Life, time
Setting sun

Life, time
Surrealist son

Life, time
Dreams unsung

Space, time
Continuum

Space, time
Oubliette

Space, time
Dancing step

Space, time
Collage concrète

Sounding like
A poppy

La Rose Impossible

Saint-Cirq
Lapopie

Bulbs

There are no bulbs in my house
All the lights are strewn with
unintentionality

I shall set all my chairs on fire
To throw shadows over my dining
table

The electricity man doesn't come
around here any more
Nobody ever knocks at my door
The roads are empty
And the street lamps are fizzing with
decay

I have a collection of elastic bands
To keep my paperclips company
Desktop formality
Scrunched up into wastepaper basket
anonymity

The repetitive hypnotics
Of raindrops' snail-slither traces
Pelted onto the sides of Victorian
pretention and gloominess
Accentuates that these streets have
seen better days

Won't talk to anyone anymore
Hold your fire, hold your own council,
hold your medicine
Hold on a minute maybe I left a bulb
in a spare drawer
No – that was a false eyeball and a
ball of string

So, when the lights go out
Come to me with a plastic bag of
bulbs
Vitamin C, a clear vinyl Karlheinz
Stockhausen
And an orange rug

And we shall dance
To the beautiful
Absurdity
Of it all

Space Marionette

I'm the detective from outer space
You've probably never seen my face
I'm the detective from outer space
Investigating another interstellar case

Fourth-dimensional criminal activity
Time stolen from the human mind
Schizoid transference crack in time
Stolen from the subject's mind

Television head at the end of the bed
Dreams given us from the unsaid
Saving the human race
From the greedhead alien race

My spaceship's maroon when it
appears
Million times tougher than a spider's
web
My dashboard's made of skulls
And I have a chrome-base feather bed

My mission is to catch the greedheads
Stop them in their tracks
My mission is to catch the greedheads
Stop them in their tracks

I'm the space... marionette

S-s-s- Slither

You're so boring
You remind me of decadent flooring
You're appalling
You're missing your calling

Dog and bonio
Don't call me dodo, fido, or Antonio
I don't work in a chippie on the
Hudson river
S-s-s- Slither

Verbal anorexia
Deficient in perplexia
Love and gore – hope to restore
Sold out in your favourite big store

Liaison fortitude
For shopping sink certitude
Leave for the hilly ground
Blue sky up and down
Leaving for the lost and found

Living for the lost and found

That is s-s-s- Sound

Fanni Tutti Hitching A Ride

Thought is one step removed from
essence
Writing is one step removed from
hand
Laughter is jokes in solid formation
Throw another penny down for the
band

Clouds are ticking time bombs
Emotions to be set on fire
Dreams we overloaded
Like druids at a funeral pyre

I wrote down some thoughts of Paris
Or Rome or in the street
A blue cigarette desire
Of turning heads we'll never meet

Bus-stop vacuum cleaners
And Fanni Tutti hitching a ride
There are no acceptable limits

And civilisation must be knocked aside

Purse-lipped Town

Dawn ripped through the morning
From the two-boat harbour
To the church at the other end
It marauded
Like dustbowl beasts
Stampeding across the plane
Until all is still and light restored

The uniform of the night dispelled
Sun creates a chequered town
Of shading and warmth
Which seems too modern a weather
condition
For this purse-lipped town
Of monochrome opinions

You Wear Your Mask Well

You wear your mask well
- Terror night trip in the
morning light

You sing your song in tune
- Melodious waves against
moonlit rocks

The bathroom mirror reflects another
you
- Cymbals crashing in a Japanese
room

Your expression reveals the truth of
your waking thoughts
- Tiny boats tumbling over foam-
white torrents

Your clothes mark you out as from
elsewhere
- Winter smoke rising from a
wooden shack on the shores of a still
lake

You are at ease amid the upturned
autumnal squalls
- Hollow laughter in a cheap motel
room

You hold your whisky glass as if
shaking hands with death
- Reflections of a clown in a
distorted circus mirror

Smoking makes the oxygen taste less
acrid
- Broken-necked guitar smouldering
on a bonfire

- Man strewn awkwardly on a bare
kitchen floor

- Concrete displacement,
greek car siren, dog yelping

- Rivulet of blood from a single nostril
- A flickering television screen
depicting the end of programming

- Books on a bookshelf and an
empty fridge
- No name, unseen

You wear your mask well
- Terror night trip in the
morning light

Francesca

Time and chance have sucked you up
into the sky
Not in a holy way
As an abstract splash of colour
As a pop-art bird with cut-up words
Cascading from its beak
As a leopard skin print
Or a stole from faux mink
Or a faded sideways-on photograph

Lobster, drummer, Dalí, daubed in red
Yellow, green, blue, egg
Velvet overground, underground,
rambling free
Speaking like melted drizzled
chocolate
In a hot coals sea

Floppy hats, bangles and rings
And many other jingly jangly things

Someone's daughter, lover, sinner,
saint
In our memories
Always surrounded by loud music
And brightly coloured paint

Innocent

I never meant to seek ablution
I never went to lick tradition
...Fifteen maidens' backs
And the crack of the bloody whip

The lampshade flickers by the wire
We could've choked on the fire
The rebel and the trees... evergreen
The damp forest... red and unseen

I am lonely   - solitary mindset

I'm a friend... walking dead

Hear the footsteps, tiptoeing lightfoot
The reasons are, the reason is
...seen gaping in the mist
...seen gaping in the mist

Been here before, and it's seemed so
meant

Been here before... innocent

Mark E. Smith

Street poet
Battered mind
Battered cod
For the real British Blues
Street fighting Can
Kicking the concrete man
In-your-face absurd-of-grace
Without the twee bits round the
edges
Alleyway cat
From piss-angled flats
And Victoria is a femme-anal
In a hit northern canal...
Situated
Next to
A posh
Chemist
A pub
And a chippie

Die yourself fitter
Die yourself fitter
Die yourself fitter...
Is he a toker or a stoker or a joker?
No!
Die yourself fitter...

Mark E-Cha-cha..... The end-arrrhh!!

Moon Cling

My Star

Has Clung

To a thousand

ceilinGs in the night

A wave to the monsTers

Before the light

SiPhoning

The spiRit

Towards

transMission

As the mOOn

Drags

PoroUs

Through

manneQuined haZe

Of fuelleD happineSs

Butterfly Moses

Artistry is not plasticity
It doesn't bounce when it's dropped

Shouting in colour
Makes you feel fuller

Appetite suppressant
Like pills and screens
As she screams in tight jeans
And throws another bucket on the fire

Butterfly Moses
Like Rembrandt and Roses
And a cloud passing over the moon

Caught with a pinhole camera
Developing obscurest
At its best:
- Obscure - obscura

The Dying Sun

I see a castle on the horizon
On the top of that distant hill
The sun and the bright yellow
meadows
Hide that I'll never be happy again

And I wish I had an illness
To help me forget my grief
I wish I had a disease
To consume all the memories

For you sucked out all the poison
From deep inside of my heart
Only to replace it with another one
Which shrouded the dying sun

All My Tomorrows

I am still struck
By the death throes
Of all my tomorrows

Lapis lazuli screams
As daytime eats
Into Auburn glow

A craving
Like chocolate dripped onto air
Strikes at memories' sudden motion
Into half-lit remembrance

And as I walk through
Majestically
The leaves grieve
And martyr themselves in front of me

For I am king for a day
This day
This long day

This long short day

Infinite Concrete Mirrors

Infinite concrete mirrors
Of crumbling circus reflections
Fat and bearded
Twenty-first century gameshow
depression
Crummy seedy coin-flipping futures
Metronomes and mellotrones
Loops of inconsequential repetition

Get a room
Get a loan
Get a bone for the dog
Whilst wallpapering over secret
peeling desires

An Old Photograph

I bought an old photograph
From a street vendor in France
A couple on a cliff by the sea
Lovers like you and me

Fifty cents for someone's life
Pictures from a forgotten time
How she adores him
On a cliff path to the skies

These smiles from strangers to me
Across time and memory
From an untold story
From a street vendor in France

I'll put it on my wall
And hope it doesn't fall
Sepia's eternal fire
Sepia's internal desire

From a street vendor in France

Dusty Digital Alarm Clocks

Time
By the digital 80s alarm clock
In the shop window
Has no meaning at all

It tells me that I'm late
Hurry hurry
Or that I'm early
It doesn't matter at all

Dust gathers around my memories
Making the sunshine last forever
Reminding us that a broken clock
Is as accurate as one that ticks on
forever

And all the stolen apples
Have rotted to the ground
As all the digital clocks
Have been sent for melt-down

We, as with our memories
And our lives
And our knowledge and hopes
As with clocks and apples
And the ticking of time
Shall also rot down to the ground
Only to be one day reborn again

Echoes Around Cliffs

Your face is the cliffs
Marked out by the sun and the shade
And the fissures from weather-beaten
time

Your voice is the wind
Which whispers through the trees

Your contentment is in the low
autumn sun
And the falling of the leaves

Your pain is the thunderclaps
Which echo around the cliffs
The storms that follow
And the overflowing banks

You are hope
Forest to forest
Your sadness is the end of summer

Cities of Dust

In the cities of dust
We hold masks to our faces
And breath in the fresh air
From a memory and a glossy
photograph

Riding the Immortality Train Track

*And the greatest shock of, these, my
final years is that he's not immortal...
Mortality throat messenger, lozenged
through the sky
Cut up into pieces and rearranged just
for f-f-f-fun*

Train tracks just for vagabonds
Hobos on the wire
Sleepless nights of vassalage
Crumpled doorbell hopelessness

In a look-a-like contest for Siamese
twins
We are always destined to come
second
To the priest bending for the polo
mint
In tight jeans at the caravan cinema

Cruising down Oxford Street for
gargoyle hide-and-seek

Tears exploding on the pavement
Like octopus brains placed onto starched collars
In noise-reduction laboratory experiment – where only madmen holler

Strength in the many and numbers for the odd
The cake is in the eating, slicing and re-piecing
Take a goblet full of liquid gold and put it in your mouth
If they hurry now they can catch the boat down south

Reams and reams of somethingness folding into night
As the spacemask starfish vanishes
Heading for the light

... And there's a countdown coming

Imprisoned

A bird in a cage
Love in a rage
People on the sidewalk
Looking like they can't talk

People are in prison
Making their decisions
Emotional precision
Love is always in transition

In Secret Moments

The song of love is alone
As the man dressed as a priest
Sings in the theatre to a full house

You who have nothing
Give me your shadow
To protect me from the silence

The day haunts us

In secret moments
Swans can be seen
Beyond the forest

Darkness and hope...
Beyond the forest
Eternity Lies

Belinka

Oh Belinka
The stars will fall from the sky
And you will eat up the moon

Oh Belinka
The clocks are covered in snow
And the trees only grow in your mind

Oh Belinka
Why is the forest so deep in snow
And how do you leave no footprints

Oh Belinka
Do you know what love is Belinka
Have you a second hand on your clock
Belinka

Oh Belinka
Sing Belinka sing
Let your dress swirl around you as you
dance to the music in your head

Oh Belinka
The factory closed ten minutes early
Is there a story there Belinka

Oh Belinka
We exist outside of our own heads
And temptation is the sundial of
expectation Belinka

Oh Belinka
Horses can breathe through their eyes
Did you know that Belinka

Oh Belinka
Let us celebrate with wine and
solitaire
And allow the people from the hollow
to eat the crows

Oh Belinka
Let us throw all the clocks into the
broken river
And let us dance

Oh Belinka
The stars will fall from the sky
And you will eat up the cosmos

Zig Zag Life

My Zigzag life
My happy life
My beautiful life
Rainy Monday life
Stormy Wednesday life
Dancing barefoot life

My zigzag existence
The wind in my hair
Sea spray on my cheeks
Wrapped up warm by hot chocolate
fires
Crisp-crunch snowmen
And melted marshmallows

France in the autumn
Sunday pubs
Pompeii at sunset
No regrets
Nick Drake's music
Soothed melancholic

Broom-brooming around
Pretending to be a car
Bumping into wardrobes
And playing guitar
Singing songs in silence
Whilst jumping into puddles

I hope this moment (these moments)
Never end
Eating bananas for breakfast
Being driven round the bend
Sitting by rivers in the pouring rain
Wondering what it's like to be insane

Oh, my zigzag life
My happy life
My beautiful life
My sunshine life
... My moonlanding
And sometimes my just still-standing...
life

A French Cigarette

Sitting under a centuries old
Covered market in France
Wood and darkened beams
Pillars and uneven flooring

A bar in the corner
And distant conversations
Too faint to make out
As the chimes of church bells ring out

The late summer sun
Sucks the chill
From the sloped,
Uneven, cobbled evening

As the mist of a French cigarette
Floats down on the breeze
To weave itself
With the dominant smells
Of spilt diesel and exotic southern
plants

The heat of the summer
Is gently giving way
To the season's change
And the preparations
For closed shutters
Smoky fires and falling leaves

A last glass of wine then held high
In the square under the covered
market
In salutation
To a summer that is nearly over

A Land of Happy Mirrors

Streams of dreams
Rippling over waterfall memories

Summers of past content
Autumning into shadows of sorrow

At the rising of the winds
Which create the formations of the
clouds
That signal an end of sorts

Summer drinks up our nostalgia
As we pretend
That the harshness of winter
Is as it always was
In the childhood of our reveries

Never forgetting
That our thoughts
Are choices
In a land of happy mirrors

79

Which balance
On the edge
Of knowing...

Untitled

Love and confusion
Cloud the trees
The wind is mystery

Fire's infinite dance
Caught
Through another's eyes

Splintered Rays

Luminosity
Rose from the ashes
Of obscurity

Beckoning
A new
Age

Like
Splintered
Rays

Through
A forest
Sunrise

Fading
Shadows
Burnt away

Along with
The morning

Haze

Signalling
That
Everything

Was finally
Going to be
Alright

Echoing Down To The River

I'm watching the clock in the hall
As the seasons fall away
And the chimes echo down to the
river

Gazing through the pane
At the wind and the rain
As the seasons come and go

There are crumbs on the floor
Leaves by the door
And a wind that chills to the bone

But I'm ready for the off
Once I'm rid of this cough
And my back aches a little less

True, I've been here for a while
With an expectant smile
My coat and scarf at the ready

But at last today is the day
For which I've been waiting so long
For life to truly begin

Dawn's Next Appearance

who got
busted in
    the supernatural darkness
   of their brains

ancient hotels staggering across
with their burning tatters
of supernatural
darkness
hysterical and naked
    they drag
their money in the unnatural gloom of
the cold-water night

as I
continued to
    peel away
     the pleasure of a
    crazed
burning
nobleman
whirling among

the scene
    that finally broke me

and the insane
fireside abandon
    allowed
  the imagination
to banquet and play
for the
 minds
were but masks
     triggered
by dawn's next appearance

Someone I Once Knew

my withering
will turn the
needless shadows
into
yesterday's wish

as my happiness
propels
delicious
mystery laughter
onto someone
I once knew

late thoughts
cool
my soon rounded
conversations
as in decadence bay
my horse-regrets
come and go

as the golden
singing me
brushes away
the recollections
from my plate
before dawn

Foreverland

The empty station's dancing echo
Reminds me of a desolate siren
Like meaningless infinity
Or staying at the wrong motel

Like a wildly mythical
Foreverland
Filled with footsteps
And sky-mirrors

As the naked train
Within someone
Hurtles through the wind
Like the ringing of distant circles

To never arrive is also something
Freed from flames
Of wilderness shorelines
And the hope of the solitary footstep

Our Impossible Improbable

Lines of silence
Reach our impossible improbable
Where forgotten stories
Echo through the wallpaper
Where they are freely rebuilt
In our wish-clouds

And the singing trees
Cannot be blustered away
For they are rooted
In our waking reflections
Our factory moonscapes
And our hushed tomorrows

We see distant backdrop mountains
Like dream angels
And pale passageways
Making the magnificence of our
meanings
Walk hand in hand with
Our lifelong invisible companions

Colours of Her Youth

So, she wonders, who built the moon
With maple syrup and a mysterious
tune
As she boards her train in a black and
white film
With sound effects from the glory
days of Italian cinema

But she cut her teeth on egg and
spoon races
And the gypsy rides
Waiting a year for the fair to come to
town
To listen to the fortune teller on
candyfloss morning

The swinging boats and the floating
ducks
And coconuts glued into holes
The bright light futility that's filled
with hope
For a plastic bag fish and a cuddly toy

Oh, the sounds and the lights
And the flashing nights
As people bounce and spin
And are then lost forever

But those dreams are gone
She's now trapped in a black and
white movie
On a steam train
Through the fog of distant times

With her elegant cigarette holder and
smudged lipstick
She barely notices the Conductor
When he comes to punch her ticket
As she gazes out of the window at the
colours of her youth

Plain Starlight

I am full now
Of the velvet fathomableness
And the strung-out decay

Dancing with trembling lunatics
In plain starlight
Reminds me of life's surface

The moon resembles greatness
Through the undone window
Of the fractured mansion

As I lie by the window
Considering life's
Prodigious regrets

Paloo Paloo

Lapa loola lapa lila lapa loola li
Fala foola fala feela fala moola ki
Jaka jaka waka waka mass-de doodi
da
Hama harma hama hoola hamer poola
pee
Paloo paloo paloo pyjama
weeeeeeeee

Notes and Acknowledgements

Moon Cling – I wrote the moment I heard that David Bowie had died.

Mark E. Smith – I wrote after hearing that the wonderful musician and lyricist had sadly died.

Paloo Paloo – is dedicated to Hugo Ball, a German author, poet, and essentially the [co-] founder of the Dada movement; and pioneer in the development of sound poetry. The poem appears in my novel *The Cubist's House*.

Francesca – is dedicated to an exceptionally unique person, character and artist who tragically died recently, far far too young.

Divinely Imperfect – is for my magical, mysterious and inspirational a.p..

Also by Jean Bonnin

Novels
A Certain Experience of the Impossible
Lines Within the Circle
The Cubist's House

Poetry/Aphorisms/Short Stories
Being and Somethingness
Un-usual Muse-uals

Translations
Magical Sense (by Malcolm de Chazal)
Magical Science (by Malcolm de
Chazal)

Edited by Jean Bonnin
The Nuremberg Trials: A Personal
History (by Georges Bonnin)

Art
A Welsh Surrealist: Jean Bonnin

Symbolists believe that art should represent absolute truths that can only be described indirectly. Thus, they write in a very metaphorical and suggestive manner, endowing particular images or objects with symbolic meaning.

V1

www.redeggpublishing.com

www.ingramcontent.com/pod-product-compliance
Lightning Source LLC
LaVergne TN
LVHW051750080426
835511LV00018B/3287